11024/Guinness Activity 2001

ACTIVITY BOOK

FOOD
☆ ☆ ☆

Marbles

??

THE NATURAL WORLD
☆ ☆ ☆

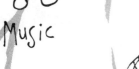

Music

Ball

MUSIC
☆ ☆ ☆

The world's largest pumpkin weighed 1,131 pounds.

Home Run!!

SPORTS
☆ ☆ ☆

Bat

COLLECTIONS
☆ ☆ ☆

ODDS & ENDS
☆ ☆ ☆

Worm   Hook   ??

Farmer

BIGGEST BUBBLE GUM BUBBLE:

Susan Montgomery Williams of Fresno, California blew the largest recorded bubble gum bubble. Its diameter measured 23 inches.

A. Bubbles
B. Bubbles
C. Bubbles
D. Bubbles
E. Bubbles
F. Bubbles
G. Bubbles
H. Bubbles
I. Bubbles
J. Bubbles

Bubble Blower

Which one is different?

Which does not belong?

Did you know?

A. Ladle

B. Rolling Pin

C. Pots and Pans

D. Food

E. Worm Hook

F.

Chef

Cook

A chef uses certain items to cook with and make different types of foods. Which of the above does not belong?

BIGGEST HAMBURGER:

The biggest hamburger ever weighed 2.7 tons and was 24 feet in diameter. Loran Green and friends from Hi Line Promotions, Malta, Montana, made it at the Saco, Montana on September 5, 1999.

FARTHEST PIZZA DELIVERY:

In March 1998, Eddie Fishbaum, the owner of Broadway's Jerusalem 2 in New York City, USA, was asked to hand-deliver a plain pizza base to TV presenter Fiji Bando in Tokyo, Japan - a distance of 6,753 miles. The request was made on the Japanese TV show "Unbelievable," shown on the Fuji network. The total cost of the pizza, including Fishbaum's expenses, came to $7,000.

FASTEST ICE CREAM EATER:

The fastest ice cream eater is Tony Dowdeswell. He ate 3 pounds 6 ounces of unmelted ice cream in 31.67 seconds in New York City in July 1986.

Fill in the blanks to finish this puzzle.
Use the last three Guinness World Records
to find the answers.

Ice Cream

Scoop

The _____ _____ ever weighed 2.7 _____
and was 24 feet in _____ .

The _____ _____ delivery was a _____ of 6,753 _____.

The _____ _____ _____ _____ is Tony Dowdeswell.

The largest hamburger is waiting for you. How fast can you get to it?

TALLEST CAKE:

In August 1997, a 105 tier, 105 foot tall cake was created by Network Television Marketing Ltd. in Faisalabad, Pakistan.

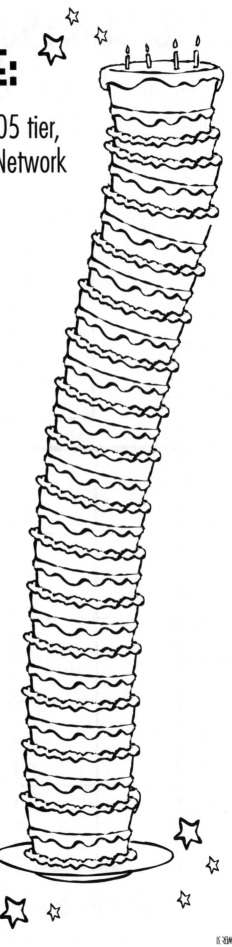

How many layers can you count on this cake ??

————————————

NUMBER OF LAYERS

How many layers can you make on your own cake ??

————————————

NUMBER OF LAYERS

MOST POPULAR FRUIT:

The banana (Musa Sapientum), together with its relative the plantain (Musa paradisiaca), is the most consumed fruit in the world.

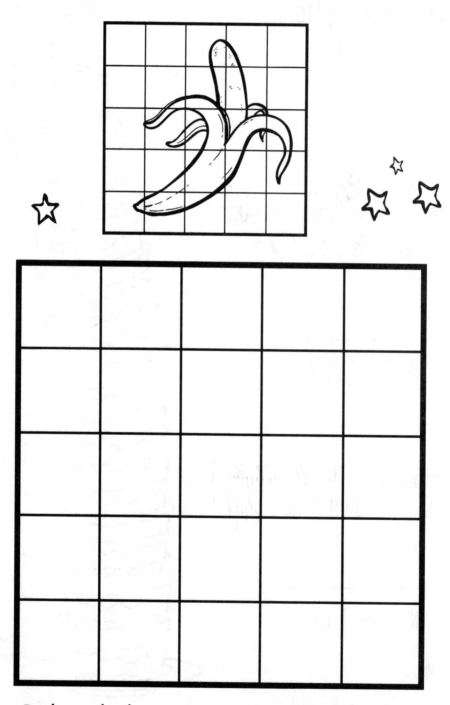

Redraw the banana using the grid as a guide.

BIGGEST ICE CREAM SUNDAE:

Did you know?

Palm Dairies Ltd., under the supervision of Mike Rogiani, made an ice cream sundae weighing 24.5 tons on July 24, 1988 in Edmonton, Alberta, Canada.

A. Chocolate Syrup

B. Scoop

C. Ice Cream

D. Rolling Pin

E. Cherry

Which does not belong?

Biggest Sundae

ANSWER: D

BIGGEST FEAST:

A record 150,000 guests attended a feast held by Alul Dalpatlal Shah to celebrate his inauguration as a monk. It took place in Ahmadabad, India on June 2, 1991.

MOST EXPENSIVE FRUIT:

Leslie Cook, a restaurant manager, paid $906 for 1 pound of strawberries. They were auctioned in Dublin, Republic of Ireland.

Did you know?

Chef

LONGEST EGG THROW:

Johnny Dell Foley threw a fresh hen's egg 323 ft. 2 in. without breaking it, on November 12, 1978, in Jewett, Texas.

Cook

WORD SEARCH:

THESE WORDS ARE FOUND IN THE LAST TWO
GUINNESS WORLD RECORD FACTS.

```
Z I T O B K O Q M B O C K F
R E X P E N S I V E O R G H
S N M R G O O C G D H I P E
T P U Q G M M F G U E S T S
F E A S T C Y L E K N N E F
R G P Y H D E L L E G N X I
E G S D R L L I S E I Y A H
S U T B O J O H N N Y H S K
H V Y T W E F M O M E T E R
I P X X W C E R V R N J U D
S Q W M P T N J U T G V U N
T A Z C O O K D O I L O K A
R F B N U O R C R N T P S L
A G E L N N B L K D N W L E
W H Y A D A N A P I D Z Y R
B E R R I E S G N A H S A I
```

WORD LIST:

FEAST	HEN	THROW
GUESTS	STRAWBERRIES	FRUIT
TEXAS	FRESH	COOK
EXPENSIVE	FOLEY	POUND
EGG	DELL	IRELAND
MONK	JOHNNY	INDIA

Cook

Redraw the hamburger using the grid as a guide.

MOST VALUABLE SLICE OF CAKE:

A piece of wedding cake from the wedding of the Duke of Windsor and Wallis Simpson sold for $29,900. It was more than 60 years old.

Which one is different ??

Create your own personal record!

Next time you have green peas for dinner, see how many you can pile on a spoon. Have a contest with your family or friends. Record the winner below. (Be sure to eat all your peas!)

Biggest Sundae

★MY★ RECORD

MOST PEAS BALANCED ON A SPOON:

_____
NAME

_____   _____
NUMBER OF PEAS   DATE

HIGHEST MOUNTAINS:

Mount Everest, in the eastern Himalayas on the Tibet-Nepal border, has a record-breaking height of 29,029 ft. It was officially recognized as the world's highest mountain in 1856, following surveys carried out by the Indian government.

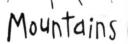

Mountains

Mountain Climber

MOST ACTIVE VOLCANO:

Kilauea, on Hawaii, USA, is the world's most active volcano. It has been erupting on a continuous basis since 1983, and discharges lava at a rate of 177 ft. per second.

Compass

Hawaiian Islands

WORD SEARCH:
THESE WORDS ARE FOUND IN THE LAST TWO
GUINNESS WORLD RECORD FACTS.

A I T D N O C E S L A P E N
C H I G H E S T T E S R G H
T N L R I V V C L D S M P E
I P L O B E G E E A T Y T S
V S I C E R R L R K V N E G
E N B O R E F E L E T A X I
E I S N K S T Y C E S Y A I
S A I A Y I O P H O E T S A
D T Y C W E L M E E R T E W
N N X L A C E A V O I D U A
R U W O H H N J U T P G U H
E O Z V O C C D T E L L H D
T M O U N T I E W O A P E T
S G E E R U P T I N G E L U
A T I B E T N A N A I D N I
E E R H I M A L A Y A S O N

WORD LIST:

HIGHEST	TIBET	VOLCANO
MOUNTAINS	NEPAL	KILAUEA
MOUNT	RECORD	HAWAII
EVEREST	HEIGHT	ERUPTING
EASTERN	INDIAN	LAVA
HIMLAYAS	ACTIVE	SECOND

BIGGEST METEORITE:

A 9-ft. 10-in. meteorite found at Hoba West, near Grootfontein, Namibia, in 1920, was estimated to weigh 58 tons.

Did you know?

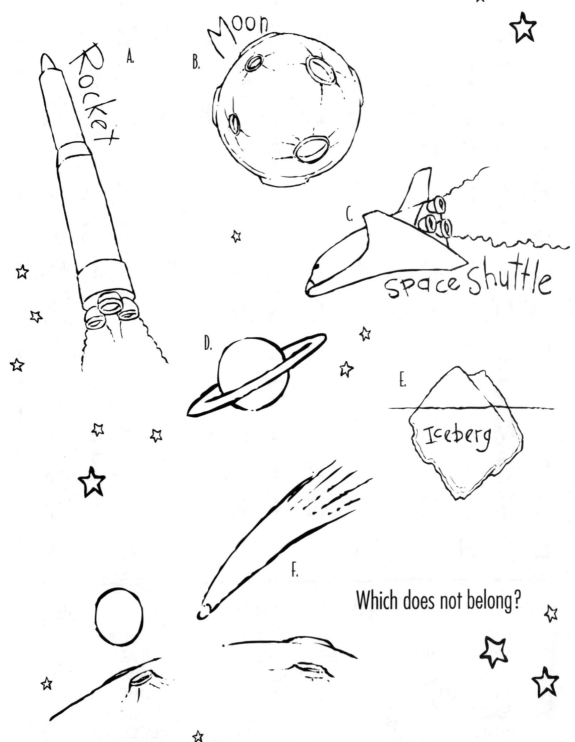

A. Rocket

B. Moon

C. Space Shuttle

D.

E. Iceberg

F.

Which does not belong?

TALLEST PERSON:

Robert Wadlow (USA) measured 8 ft. 11- 1/10 inches tall in 1940, shortly before his death.

Did you Know?

Tallest Man

Which one is different?

ANSWER: E

OLDEST ASTRONAUT IN SPACE:

John Glenn, Jr. was the oldest astronaut to visit space in October 1998 at the age of 77!

What do you think space looks like?
Draw and color it.

Astronaut

SMALLEST OCEAN:

The world's smallest ocean is the Arctic Ocean, which has a surface area of 5,105,700 miles.

A. Igloo

B. Igloo

C. Igloo

D. Igloo

E. Igloo

F. Igloo

The Smallest ← Ocean

G. Igloo

H. Igloo

I. Igloo

J. Igloo

K. Igloo

Which igloo is different?

MOST RAINY DAYS:

Mt. Waialeale on Kauai, Hawaii, USA, has up to 350 rainy days per year.

Hawaiian Islands

Redraw the picture using the grid as a guide.

LARGEST PUMPKIN GROWN:

Gerry Checkon of Altoona, Pennsylvania, USA, grew the world's largest pumpkin. It weighed 1,131 pounds on October 2, 1999.

How big do you think this pumpkin could be?
Draw and color it.

BIGGEST FEET:

Excluding cases of elephantiasis, the biggest feet currently known are those of Matthew McGrory of Pennsylvania, USA, who wears a record size 28.5 shoes.

Did you know?

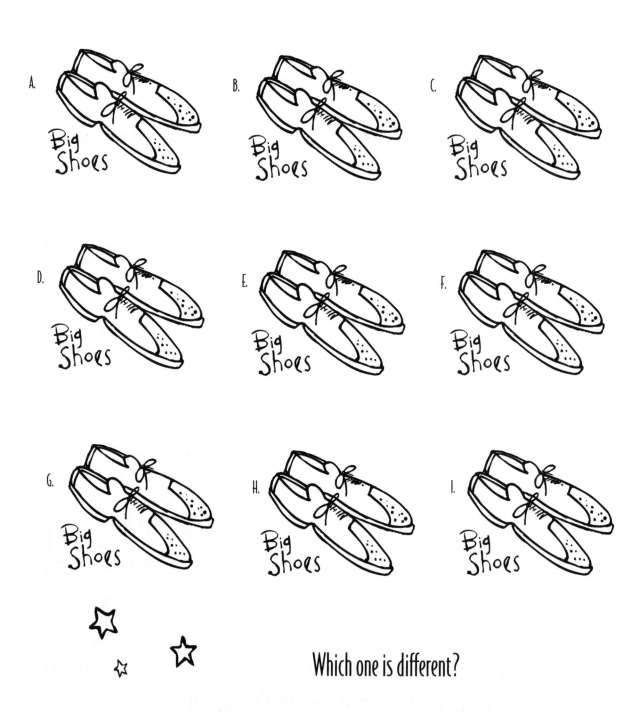

A. Big Shoes

B. Big Shoes

C. Big Shoes

D. Big Shoes

E. Big Shoes

F. Big Shoes

G. Big Shoes

H. Big Shoes

I. Big Shoes

Which one is different?

WOW!
He's
Tall!

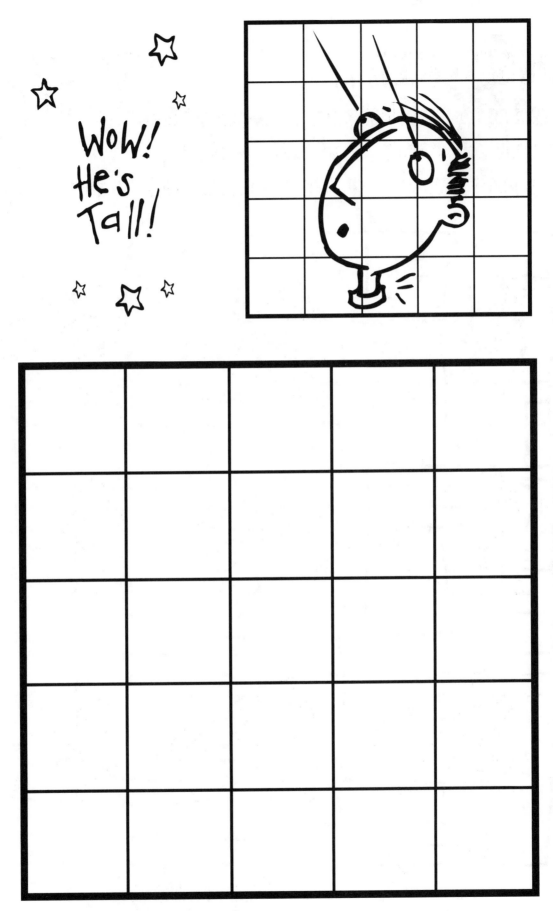

Redraw the picture using the grid as a guide.

FIRST PERSON TO CLIMB MT. EVEREST:

Did you know?

In May of 1953, Edmund Hillary was the first person to climb and reach the summit of Mt. Everest (29,029 ft.).

A. Boots

B. olympics

C. Mountains

Which does not belong?

Mountain Climber

D. Gloves

E. Oxygen tank

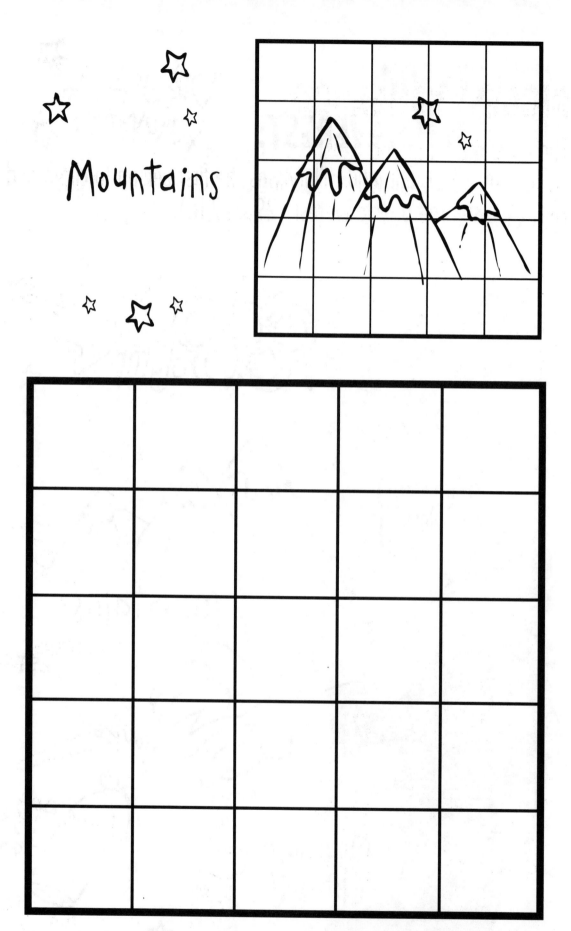

Mountains

Redraw the mountains using the grid as a guide.

BIGGEST KANGAROO:

The male red kangaroo (Australia) measures up to 5 ft. 11 in. tall when standing, and has a total length (including tail) of 9 ft. 4 in. It can weigh up to 198 lbs.

Did you know?

Which does not belong?

A. Australia

Marsupials have Pockets or

B. Pouches

Biggest Kangaroo

Tornado

C.

D. Tape Measure

E. Boomerang

NEAREST STAR:

The nearest star visible to the naked eye is the Southern hemisphere binary Alpha Centauri, which is 4.40 light years distant.

LONGEST REEF:

Australia

The Great Barrier Reef, situated off the coast of Queensland, Australia, stretches a total distance of 1,260 miles. Over 500 islands make up the reef. These islands are home to many species of birds, fish, turtles, stingrays, sea anemones and over 340 species of coral.

What do you think the Great Barrier Reef looks like?
Draw and color it.

FASTEST TORNADO:

The highest speed measured to date in a tornado is 280 m.p.h., at Wichita Falls, Texas, USA, on April 2, 1958.

MOST INTENSE RAINFALL:

On Nov. 26, 1970, a record 1.5 inches of rain fell in one minute at Basse Terre, Guadaloupe.

LOWEST TEMPERATURE:

The lowest natural temperature reliably recorded on the Earth's surface was -128.6 degrees Fahrenheit, measured at Vostok, Antarctica, on July 21, 1983.

Tornado

Rain

Igloo

Fill in the blanks to finish this puzzle.
Use the last three Guinness World Records to find the answers.

The ___1___ ___2___ ___3___ to date in a ___4___ is 280 m.p.h., at Wichita Falls Texas, USA, on April 2, 1958.

The most ___5___ ___6___ was in Base Terre, Guadaloupe on Nov, 26, 1970, a record 1.5 in of ___7___ fell in one ___8___.

The ___9___ ___10___ ___11___ recorded on the ___12___ ___13___ was -128.6 ___14___ F. at Vostok, Antarctica, on July 21, 1983.

Create your own personal record!

Ruler →

Who has the biggest foot? Have a contest with your family and friends. Use a large piece of blank paper. Close to the bottom of the page draw a line with a pencil. Have each person stand barefoot on the paper lining up each heel with the line. Make a mark at the top of their longest toe. Use a ruler to measure the winning foot!

★MY★ RECORD

BIGGEST FOOT:

_____
NAME

_____   _____
FOOT MEASUREMENT   DATE

GUINNESS WORLD RECORDS

MUSIC

Did you know?

Drum

Music

The most successful group is The Beatles.

Record

Rock and Roll

BEST SELLING ALBUM:

Did you know?

"Thriller" by Michael Jackson is the best seller of all time. The global sales since 1982 total over 47 million copies.

Music

HIGHEST-EARNING POP STAR:

Celine Dion's income of $55.5 million made her the highest-earning pop star in a single year. Her successes include "My Heart Will Go On", the theme from "Titanic". (USA, 1997)

BEST-SELLING ALBUM BY A TEENAGE SOLO ARTIST:

By February 2000, "...Baby One More Time" by Britney Spears had sold over 12 million copies in the USA.

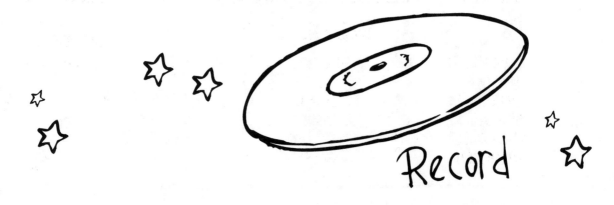

Record

WORD SEARCH:

THESE WORDS ARE FOUND IN THE LAST THREE
GUINNESS WORLD RECORDS FACTS.

```
Z I T O B Z O Y E N T I R B
R E T H R I L L E R O R G H
S T M R G H O C S P E A R S
T S U J A C K S O N E E L K
Q E A N E C A T E K R N C F
W B P L S O Z A T E G N E I
O V T D B L O R S E I Y L H
K U E B C U G N F G H H I K
C V E T H E M I L L I O N R
I P N S W C I M V R N J E C
L Q A E Y T C J E T P V U I
A A G H C I H I N C O M E N
B D E G A O A C R H P P S A
O I R I D N E L K A N W L T
L O Y H W A L A P U S A Y I
G N I L L E S G N I H S A T
```

WORD LIST:

THRILLER
BEST
SELLING
ALBUM
MICHAEL
JACKSON

GLOBAL
MILLION
CELINE
DION
INCOME
HIGHEST
TITANIC

Record

POP
STAR
TEENAGER
SPEARS
BRITNEY
USA

Electric Guitar

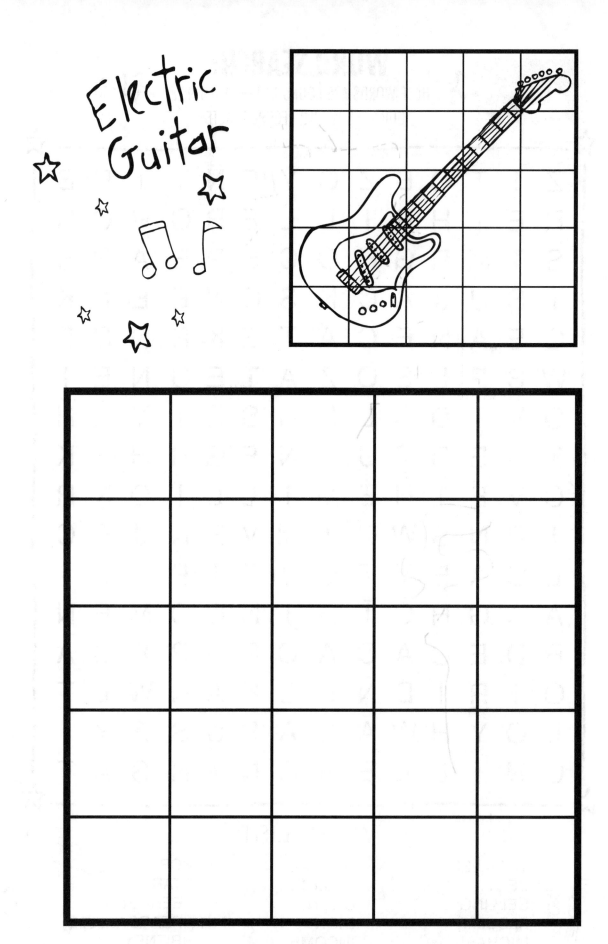

Redraw the guitar using the grid as a guide.

YOUNGEST OPERA SINGER:

Did you know?

USA opera singer Ginetta La Bianca was 15 years, 316 days old when she sang the role of Gilda in Verdi's Rigoletto in Belletri, Italy, on March 24, 1950.

Which does not belong?

Opera Singer

A. Italy

B. The Opera Program

C. Mask

D. Music

E. Stage

ANSWER: C

START

FINISH

Drum

FASTEST DRUMMER:

Rory Blackwell of Great Britain played a total of 400 separate drums in a time of 16.2 seconds. Can you finish this maze to beat his time?

BIGGEST
ROCK CONCERT ATTENDANCE:

Rod Stewart's free concert at Copacabana Beach, Rio de Janeiro, Brazil, on New Year's Eve, 1994, reportedly attracted an audience of 3.5 million.

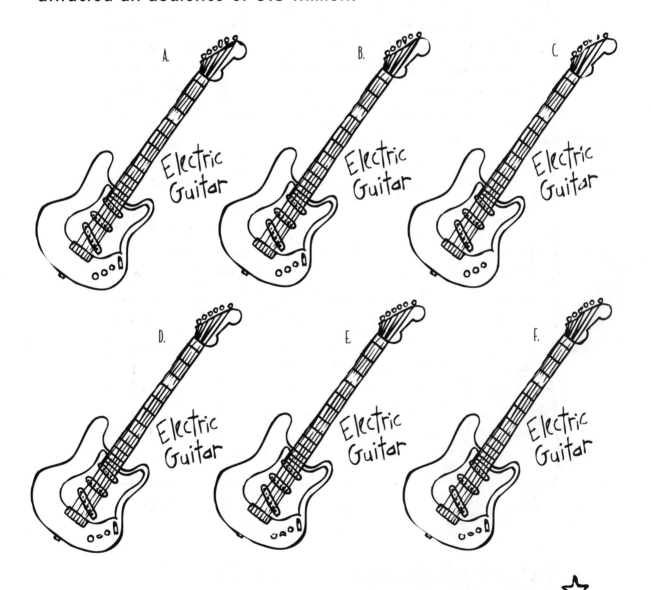

A. Electric Guitar
B. Electric Guitar
C. Electric Guitar
D. Electric Guitar
E. Electric Guitar
F. Electric Guitar

Which guitar is different?

ANSWER: C

MOST VALUABLE GUITAR:

One of Eric Clapton's guitars, a Fender Stratocaster "Brownie", earned $497,500 at a charity auction.

A. AMP

Which does not belong?

B. Music

C. Film

D. Electric Guitar

E. Pick

Guitar Player

ANSWER: C

LOUDEST AND LARGEST MUSICAL INSTRUMENT:

The loudest and largest musical instrument ever made is the now partially functional Auditorium Organ in Atlantic City, New Jersey. Its volume equals that of 25 brass bands.

What do you think this instrument looks like?
Draw and color it.

Music

MOST SUCCESSFUL COUNTRY ARTIST:

Garth Brooks is the most successful country recording artist of all time. His album sales total 92 million dollars.

BEST SELLING JAZZ ARTIST:

USA saxophonist Kenny G has sold an estimated 55 million albums worldwide. This includes "Breathless", the best-selling jazz album of all time, selling an estimated 14 million copies.

Which AMP is different?

Fill in the blanks to finish this puzzle.
Use the last two Guinness World Records
to find the answers.

Record

Music

Guitar

Garth ^{1.}_____ is the most ^{2.}_____ ^{3.}_____

^{4.}_____ ^{5.}_____ of all time .

Kenny G has ^{6.}_____ an estimated 55 million ^{7.}_____ ^{8.}_____.

BIGGEST-SELLING SALSA ARTIST:

Marc Anthony (USA) is the top selling tropical salsa artist in the world. "I Need To Know," from his fourth album sold over one million copies in the USA, reaching the Top 10 there and in Canada.

What if you were a top selling musical performer?
Draw a picture of your CD cover.

Music

START

FINISH

Record

MOST WEEKS AT
NO. 1 ON THE US SINGLES CHART:
The longest chart-topper since 1955 has
been "I Will Always Love You" by Whitney Houston, which was
No. 1 for 14 weeks in 1992.

MOST SUCCESSFUL GROUP:

The most successful group is The Beatles. They sold about 1 billion records, had a record 20 number-one singles and 18 number-one albums in the US and 17 number-one singles and 14 number-one albums in the UK.

Using the one word given, finish the puzzle using words related to The Beatles.

WORD LIST: RINGO, JOHN, GEORGE, PAUL, RECORDS, ROCK, STARS, GUITAR, ROLL

BIGGEST DRUM:

The biggest drum has a diameter of 15 ft. 6 in. and a depth of 6 ft. 3 in. It was first played at the St. Patrick's Festival in Dublin, Ireland, on March 13, 1999, to mark the launch of Ireland's Millennium festivals.

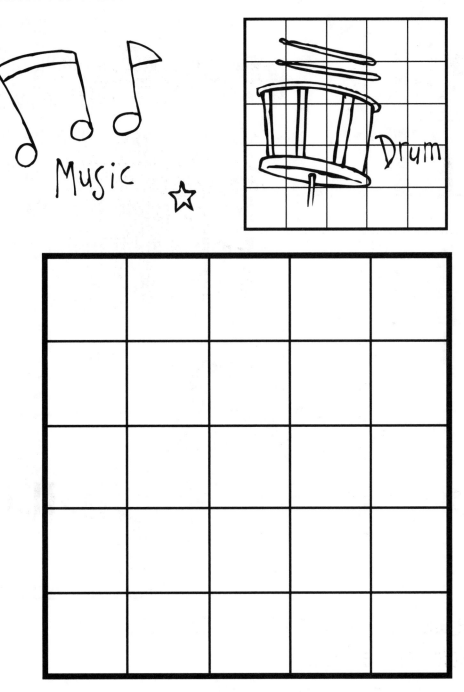

Redraw the drum using the grid as a guide.

Guitar Player

AMP

> ## Create your own personal record!

How many bands, singers and musicians can you think of? Have a contest with your family or friends. On a blank piece of paper write down all the musical entertainers that you can think of. Record the winner with the most correct answers below.

★ MY ★
RECORD

MOST MUSICAL ENTERTAINERS LIST:

☆ _____ ☆

NAME

_____ ☆ _____

NUMBER OF MUSICAL ENTERTAINERS   DATE

MOST OLYMPIC DIVING MEDALS:

The most medals won is five, by Klaus Dibiasi of Italy (three gold and two silver from 1964 to 1976); and Greg Louganis of the USA (four gold and one silver in 1976, 1984, and 1988.)

Sproing

Diver

YOUNGEST OLYMPIC TRACK-AND-FIELD CHAMPION:

The youngest gold medalist in a track-and-field event was Babara Jones(USA.) She was 15 years, 123 days old when she ran in the winning 4x100-m. relay team at Helsinki, Finland, in July 1952.

Medal

MOST MEN'S OLYMPIC TITLES:

The USA has won a record 11 men's Olympic titles since basketball was introduced to the Games in 1936. To date, they have lost just two of their Olympic games, both of them to the USSR.

olympics

WORD SEARCH:

THESE WORDS ARE FOUND IN THE LAST THREE GUINNESS WORLD RECORDS FACTS.

```
Z I D N A L N I F B O C K W
I M O S T G E R A T O R O H
K N L R G H O C G D V N P E
N P Y B A S K E T B E E T F
I D M E D A L S E A R N I I
S L P Y T D T G T L G N T V
L O I D C L I S S L I Y L E
E G C B H L G V E G H H E K
H V Y T W E R M I G E T S R
I P X X Y C E M V N N J U S
C H A M P I O N E T G U U Q
H A Z Z A I A T O B L O O T
T F I E L D R C R H A P S Y
U G E L W N R E L A Y W L X
O H S I L V E R P S C Z Y N
T E A M Z O T G N I H K A W
```

WORD LIST:

MOST	GOLD	RELAY
OLYMPIC	SILVER	TEAM
DIVING	YOUNGEST	HELSINKI
MEDALS	TRACK	FINLAND
WON	FIELD	TITLES
FIVE	CHAMPION	BASKETBALL

olympics

MOST GRAND SLAMS:

Lou Gehrig, of the New York Yankees, hit 23 grand slams from 1923 to 1939!

A. Hat

B. Hat

C. Hat

D. Hat

E. Hat

F. Hat

G. Hat

H. Hat

I. Hat

J. Hat

Strike three! yer' out!!

Which one is different?

ANSWER: G

MOST HULA HOOPS SPUN:

Lori Lynn Lomeli (USA) spun the most hula hoops simultaneously between the shoulder and hips. She achieved a total of 82 hoops, each of which completed three full revolutions. This feat was accomplished on August 5, 1999, at the Atlantis Casino Resort in Reno, Nevada.

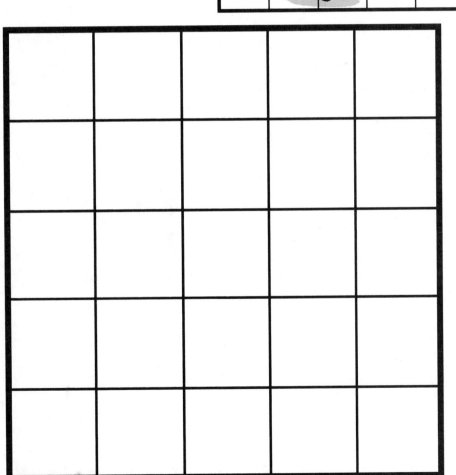

Redraw the hula hooper using the grid as a guide.

LARGEST RAINBOW TROUT CAUGHT:

David Robert White caught the largest Rainbow Trout at Bell Island in Alaska. It was caught on June 22, 1970 and weighed 42 pounds, 2 ounces.

MOST TOUCHDOWNS:

Jerry Rice (San Francisco '49ers) made 180 touchdowns in the NFL games betwen 1985 and 1999.

Did you know?

Helmet

Which football team is your favorite?
Decorate and color this helmet.

LONGEST HOME RUN:

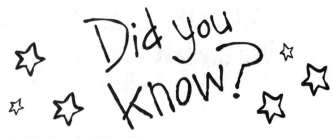

The record for the longest measured home run in a major league game is 634 ft. It was hit by Mickey Mantle for the New York Yankees (AL) against the Detroit Tigers (AL) at Briggs Stadium, Detroit, Michigan, USA on Sept. 10, 1960.

MOST HOME RUNS:

Hank Aaron holds the major league career record with 755 home runs: 733 for the Milwaukee Braves (NL, 1954-65)and Atlanta Braves, (NL, 1966-74), and 22 for the Milwaukee Brewers (AL, 1975-76.)

Fill in the blanks to finish this puzzle.
Use the last two Guinness World Records to find the answers.

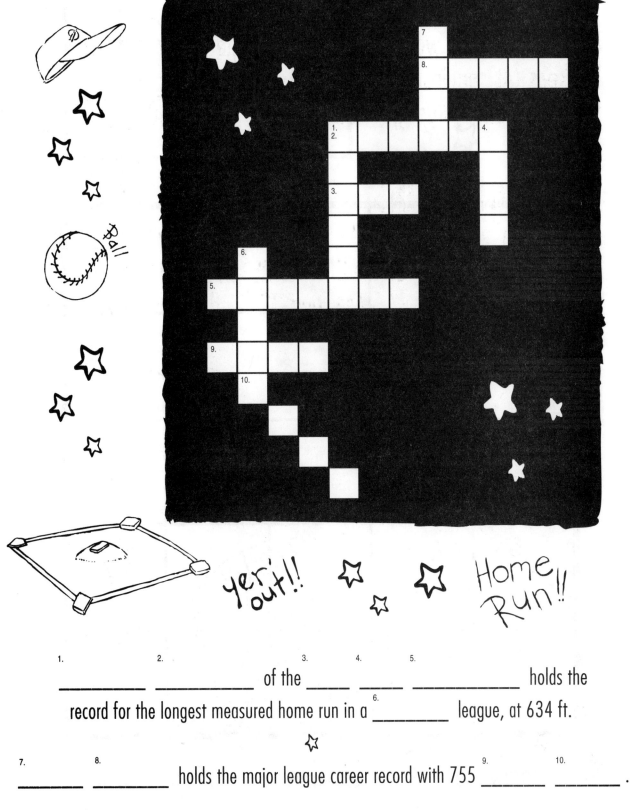

yer' out!!

Home Run!!

1. _____ 2. _____ of the 3. _____ 4. _____ 5. _____ holds the
record for the longest measured home run in a 6. _____ league, at 634 ft.

7. _____ 8. _____ holds the major league career record with 755 9. _____ 10. _____.

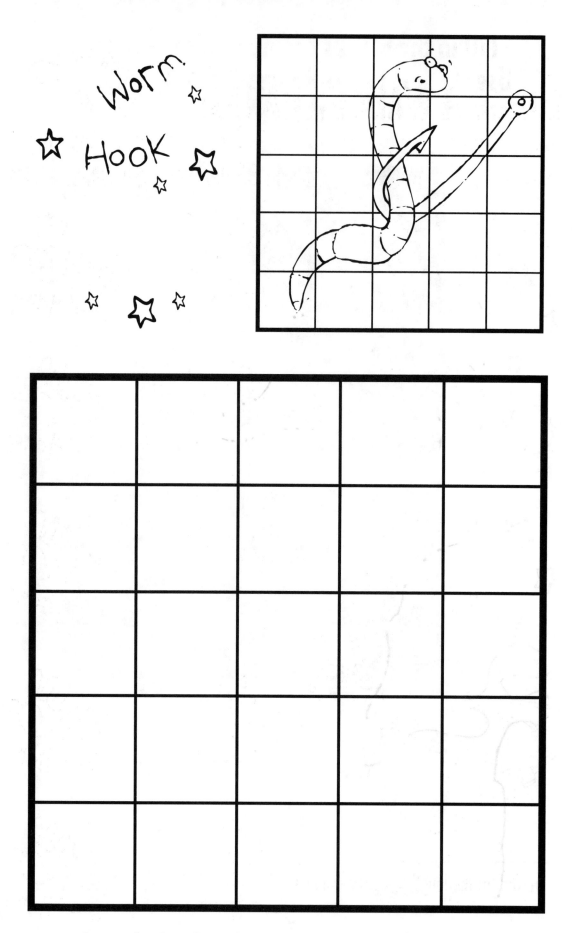

Worm.
HOOK

Redraw the hook and worm using the grid as a guide.

LONGEST WALK ON HANDS:

Did you know?

Johann Hurlinger (Austria) walked 870 miles on his hands from Vienna, Austria, to Paris, France, in 55 daily 10-hour stints.

A. Hands

B. Hands

C. Hands

D. Hands

E. Hands

F. Hands

Walking on Hands

G. Hands

H. Hands

I. Hands

J. Hands

K. Hands

L. Hands

Which hands are different?

LONGEST FIELD GOAL:

Tom Dempsey, of the New Orleans Saints, set the record for the longest field goal kicked, 63 yards. The record goal was set on November 8, 1970, while playing against the Detroit Lions.

YOUNGEST OLYMPIC GOLD MEDALIST:

Marjorie Gestring (USA) took the springboard diving title at the age of 13 years, 268 days at the Olympic Games in Berlin, Germany, August 12, 1936.

Sproing

Diver

A. Olympics

Gold Medal B.

Which does not belong?

C.

Pool

D.

E. Helmet

Berlin, Germany

Paris, France

Walking on Hands

Help Johann Hurlinger find his way to France.

Football Player

What is your favorite sport?

Draw a picture of yourself participating in your favorite sport. Do you think that you could set a Guinness World Record in it? If so, what sport would it be? _____

Create your own personal record!

Have your own Hula Hoop Contest! First, round up your friends and family. Grab a Hula Hoop. Take turns or everyone can Hula Hoop together.

Practice, practice and practice some more! The person with the most spins without a break gets the record.

100, 101, 102, 103............

★MY★
RECORD

MOST HULA HOOP SPINS:

_____
NAME

_____   _____
NUMBER OF HULA HOOPS SPUN   DATE

BIGGEST FRUIT STICKER COLLECTION:

Antoine Secco of Bourbon-Laancy, France, has collected over 20,500 different fruit stickers.

Apple

BIGGEST BARBIE DOLL COLLECTION:

Tony Mattia of Brighton, E. Sussex, England, has a collection of 1,125 Barbie dolls, about half the models produced since Mattel launched the doll in the USA in 1959.

Book

BIGGEST SIGNED BOOK COLLECTION:

Michael Silverbrooke and Pat Tonkin of Vancouver, Canada, have collected a total of 318 books that have been signed by their authors.

Did you know?

Fill in the blanks to finish this puzzle. Use the last three Guinness World Records to find the answers.

The _____ _____ _____ of Tony Mattia from England is the _____. He owns almost half the models produced by _____.

Antoine Secco of Bourbon-Laancy, France, has the largest collection of _____ _____.

The largest signed _____ collection has 318 books _____ by their _____.

BIGGEST FAKE MASTERPIECE COLLECTION:

Did you know?

Christophe Petyt of France owns over 2,500 fake paintings, representing some of the most famous works in art history.

A. Paint

B. Canvas / Easel

C. Hammer

D. Still-Life

E. Smock

F. Brushes

Which does not belong?

Painter

ANSWER: C

BIGGEST
BUS TICKET COLLECTION:

Did you know?

Yacov Yosipovv of Tel Aviv, Israel, has over 14,000 used bus tickets, every one different in some way.

Choose someplace you would like to visit.
Draw a picture of what you think this bus ticket would look like.

BIGGEST COLORED VINYL RECORD COLLECTION:

Allessandro Benedetti of Monsummano Terme, Italy, has collected 780 records made from colored vinyl.

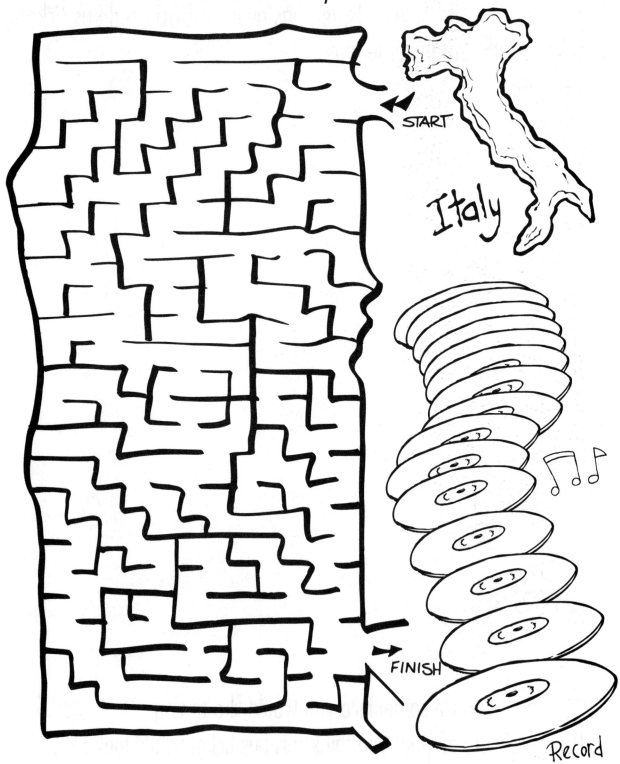

START

Italy

FINISH

Record

BIGGEST GUM COLLECTION:

The biggest bubble gum and chewing gum collection is owned by Steve Fletcher of London, England. He has collected 5,100 total packs of gum since 1980.

Did you know?

POP!

Bubbles

A. B. C. D. E. F. G. H. I. J. K. L.

Which one is different?

BIGGEST CHIP PACK COLLECTION:

Frank Ritter (USA), who lives in Nottingham, England, has collected 683 individual chip packs, from 15 different countries, since 1993.

Which does not belong?

A. Chip

B. Bag of Chips

C. Potato

D. Scoop

E. Dip

Chip Bag Collector

Did you know?

ANSWER: D

BIGGEST SHOE COLLECTION:

Sonja Bata of Toronto, Canada, has collected 10,000 pairs of shoes over a period of 50 years.

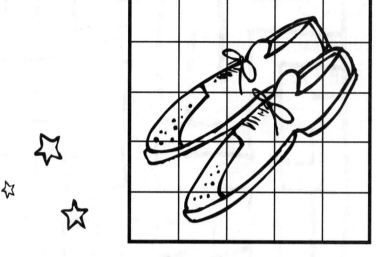

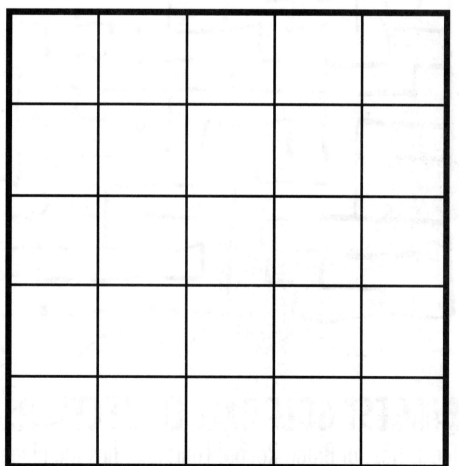

Redraw the shoes using the grid as a guide.

Did you know?

BIGGEST GOLF BALL COLLECTION:

Ted J. Hoz, of Baton Rouge, Louisiana, has the biggest golf ball collection. He has 46,778 different logo golf balls.

FAKE MASTERPIECE.

Did you know?

Find a picture of a masterpiece that you like. Using this canvas see how closely you can fake the painting.

BIGGEST REFRIGERATOR MAGNET COLLECTION:

Louisa Greenfarb, of Spanaway, Washington, USA, has collected over 29,000 refrigerator magnets.

Did you know?

BIGGEST THERMOMETER COLLECTION:

John Thynne of Southwick, W. Sussex, England, has collected 240 thermometers since 1989.

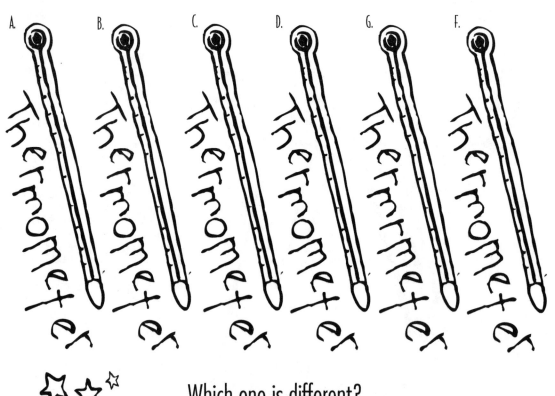

Which one is different?

WORD SEARCH:

THESE WORDS ARE FOUND IN THE LAST TWO
GUINNESS WORLD RECORDS FACTS.

```
Z  I  T  O  B  Z  O  Q  M  B  O  C  K  L
R  E  F  R  I  G  E  R  A  T  O  R  G  O
S  N  M  R  G  H  O  C  G  D  V  I  P  U
T  P  L  Q  G  B  M  F  N  J  E  E  L  I
Q  G  O  N  E  C  A  L  E  K  R  N  M  S
W  R  U  Y  S  O  Z  G  T  E  G  N  J  A
O  E  I  D  T  L  O  I  S  E  I  Y  J  H
K  E  S  B  C  L  G  N  F  G  H  H  I  K
C  N  A  T  H  E  R  M  O  M  E  T  E  R
I  F  X  X  W  C  E  M  V  R  N  J  U  S
W  A  W  M  Y  T  N  J  E  T  G  V  U  Q
H  R  Z  Z  C  I  A  D  O  B  L  O  K  T
T  B  B  N  A  O  R  C  R  H  A  P  S  M
U  G  E  L  D  N  B  L  K  A  N  W  L  X
O  H  Y  A  W  A  N  A  P  S  D  Z  Y  N
S  O  I  J  N  O  T  G  N  I  H  S  A  W
```

WORD LIST:

REFRIGERATOR	SOUTHWICK
MAGNETS	GREENFARB
LOUISA	SPANAWAY
COLLECTION	WASHINGTON
THERMOMETER	OVER
BIGGEST	THYNNE
ENGLAND	JOHN

England

Book

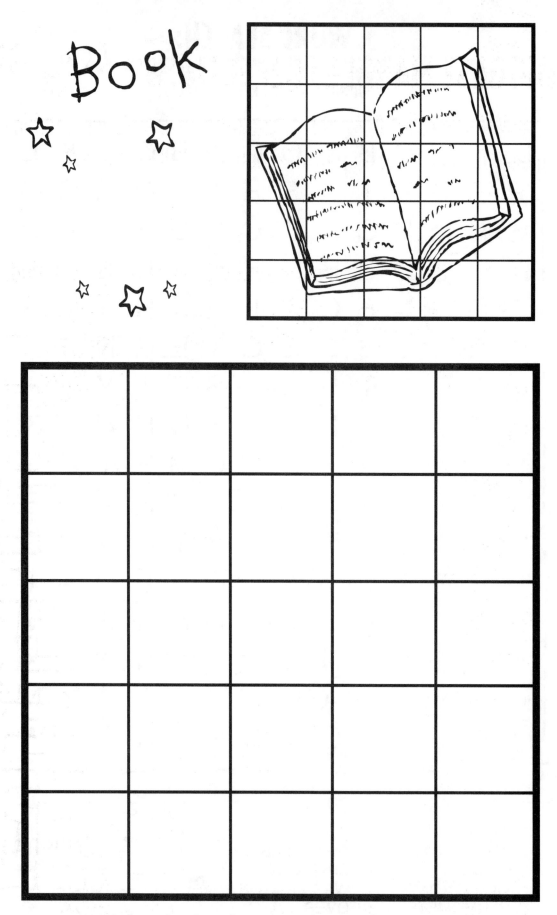

Redraw the book using the grid as a guide.

BIGGEST MARBLE COLLECTION:

Sam McCarthy-Fox of Worthing, England has the biggest marble collection. He has built up a collection of 40,000 marbles.

Count how many more marbles you find.

England

START

_____

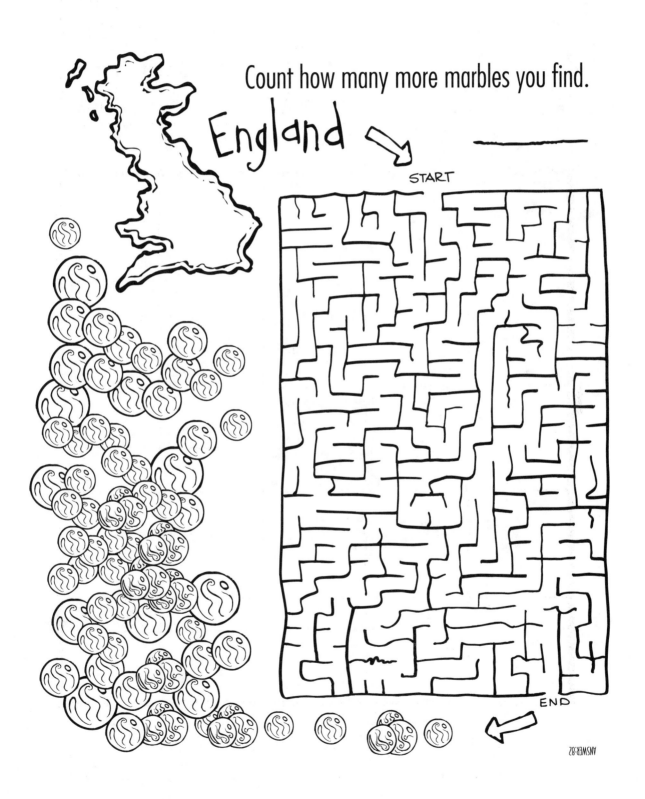

END

Marble Collection

Create your own personal record!

Do you have a collection? If you do, record it in "My Record". If you don't, why not start one? In time, maybe you can be a Guinness World Records Winner!

Marbles   Smack

SUGGESTIONS: Dolls, teddy bears, trains, marbles, popsicle sticks, crayons, pencils (Anything can be a collection. It will be more fun if it's something you really like.)

★MY★ RECORD

MY PERSONAL COLLECTION:

—————————————————
NAME

———————————   ———————
TYPE OF COLLECTION / NUMBER IN COLLECTION   DATE

BIGGEST GIFT:

The Statue of Liberty was a gift from the people of France to the USA. The statue stands 151 ft., 1 in. tall and weighs 225 tons.

BIGGEST FUNDRAISING CHARITY:

From 1991 to 1998, the US arm of the Salvation Army raised more funds annually than any other charity. Its total for 1998 was $1.2 billion.

BIGGEST SINGLE PRIVATE CHARITABLE DONATION:

Bill Gates and his wife Melinda donated a record $6 billion to The Bill & Melinda Gates Foundation in Aug 1999.

Did you know?

Statue of Liberty

Gift

WORD SEARCH:

THESE WORDS ARE FOUND IN THE LAST THREE GUINNESS WORLD RECORD FACTS.

```
Z I T O N O I T A V L A S F
R E X D L N G A T E S R G H
S N L R I O O C G D S M P E
T P L O B I G G E S T Y T S
F E I C E C I L E K A N E G
Y G B E R D F L L E T N X N
E T S R T L T Y S E U Y A I
S U I B Y J O P P N E H S S
D V Y R W E D M E E E T E I
E P X X A C E O V O N J U A
S Q W M H H N J N T P V U R
I A Z C O C C D T A L L K D
A F B T H G I E W O T P E N
R G E L N N B L K D N E L U
E C N A R F N A P I D S D F
B E R R I E S B I L L I O N
```

WORD LIST:

BIGGEST	WEIGHT	RAISED
GIFT	TONS	BILLION
STATUE	FUNDRAISING	BILL
LIBERTY	CHARITY	GATES
PEOPLE	SALVATION	DONATED
FRANCE	ARMY	RECORD

BIGGEST ROCKET:

The biggest rocket ever built was "Saturn 5", which was 363 ft. high with the "Apollo" spacecraft on top. It weighed 2,857 tons on the launchpad and had a thrust of 3,392 tons.

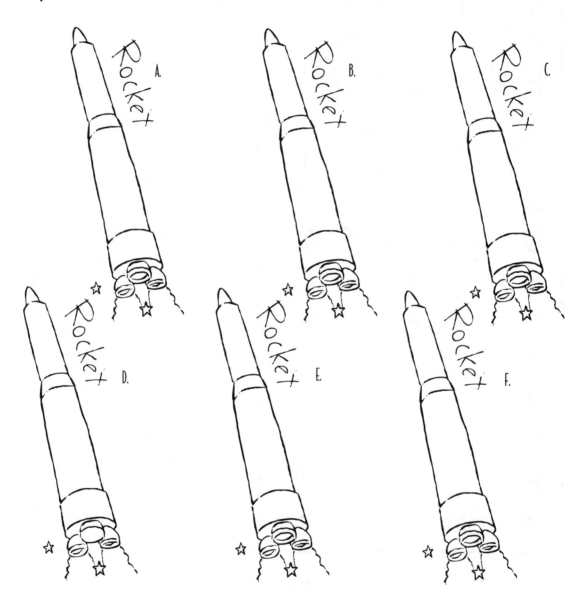

Which rocket is different?

BIGGEST ART COMPETITION:

The Winsor & Newton Millennium Painting Competition, held from 1997 to 1999, attracted a record total of 22,367 entries from amateur and professional artists in 51 countries.

Redraw the objects needed to paint a picture, using the grid as a guide.

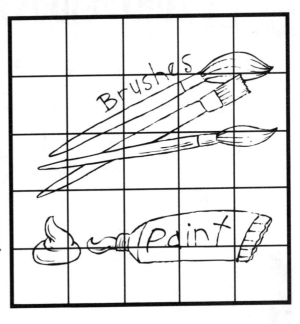

Painter

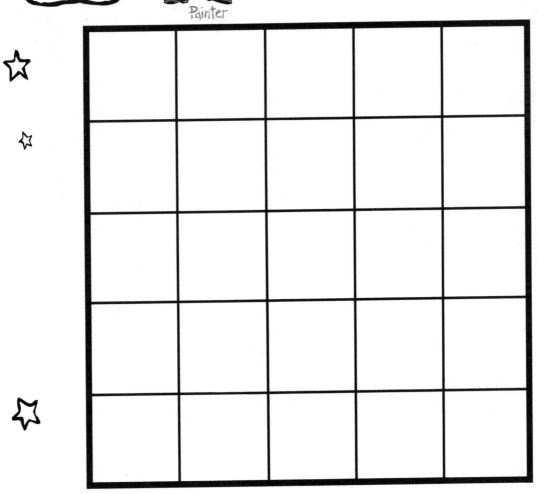

MOST COMMON CONTAGIOUS DISEASE:

Did you know?

The cold, caused by a group of at least 180 rhinoviruses, is the most common infectious disease. The condition is almost universal.

Which does not belong?

A. Mask

B. Thermometer

C. Rain

D.

E. Medicine

F. Say Ahhh

G. Xray Stethescope

Doctor

ANSWER: C

Igloo

START

FINISH

BIGGEST IGLOO:
The Ice Hotel in Jukkasjarvi, Sweden, has a record total floor area of 32,292 ft. and can sleep up to 150 hotel guests per night.

CHEAPEST CARS:

Early models of the US King Midget cars, which were made in kit form for self-assembly, sold for as little as $100 in 1948. Today, this would be equivalent to around $800.

Did you know?

Which one is different?

mechanic

HIGHEST GROSSING HORROR FILM:

The highest grossing horror film is "The Sixth Sense" (USA,1999). This film made $679.4 million worldwide by April 2000.

A. Scream!!

B. Film

C. Soda

Which does not belong?

Scary Movie

D.

Tickets

E. PopCorn

ANSWER: D

OLDEST PERSON IN SPACE:

John Glenn, Jr. was the oldest astronaut to visit space in October 1998 at the age of 77!

FIRST PERSON ON THE MOON:

On July 20, 1969, Neil Armstrong (USA), the command pilot of the Apollo 11 mission, became the first person to set foot on the Moon.

Did you know?

space Shuttle

Moon

Astronaut

Fill in the blanks to finish this puzzle.
Use the last two Guinness World Records
☆ ☆ to find the answers. ☆ ☆

1. _____ 2. _____ 3. _____ 4. _____ 5. _____ , Jr. was the _____ _____ to visit_____

6. in _____ 1998 at the age of 77.

The 7. _____ 8. _____ to set 9. _____ on the 10. _____ was 11. _____

12. _____ (USA). This command 13. _____ of the 14. _____ 11 mission

walked on the moon July 20, 1969.

MOST PARTICIPANTS IN A TV QUIZ:

The All-Japan High School quiz championship, which was televised by NTV on December 31, 1983, had a record 80,799 participants.

Did you know?

Which one is different?

Reporter

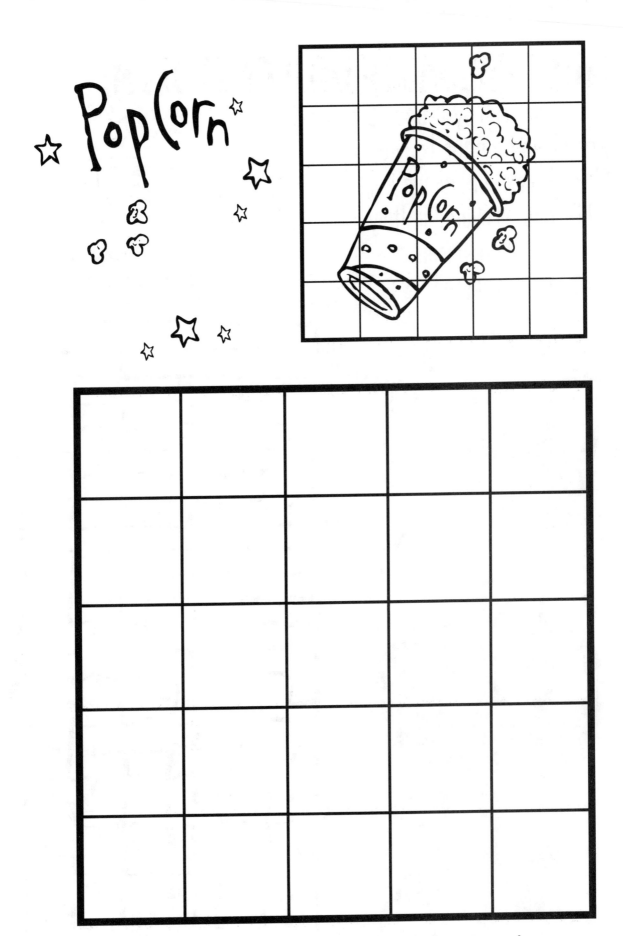

Redraw the popcorn using the grid as a guide.

MOST VALUABLE OBJECT STOLEN:

The Mona Lisa, by Leonardo da Vinci, was taken from the Louvre, Paris, France, on August 21, 1911 and recovered in Italy in 1913, when Vincenzo Perugia was charged with its theft.

MOST EXPENSIVE SHOES SOLD AT AUCTION:

On May 24, 2000, the red slippers worn by Judy Garland in "The Wizard of Oz" (1939) sold for $666,000 at Christie's in New York.

Did you know?

A. Toto

B.

Which does not belong?

C. Soda

D. Ruby Slippers

E. Witch's Hat and Broom

ANSWER: C

LONGEST LESSON:

Szabolcs Zalay, Hungary, taught a Hungarian Language and Literature lesson that lasted 24 hours, from June 18 to 19, 1999. It was attended by 34 students.

Apple

What was your longest lesson?
Draw and color what it was about.

Report Card

A-
B+
C
A
A+

Teacher

HIGHEST PRICE PAID FOR TV RIGHTS TO A FILM:

The Fox network paid $80 million for the TV rights to Steven Spielberg's "The Lost World: Jurassic Park" in June 1997, before its international release.

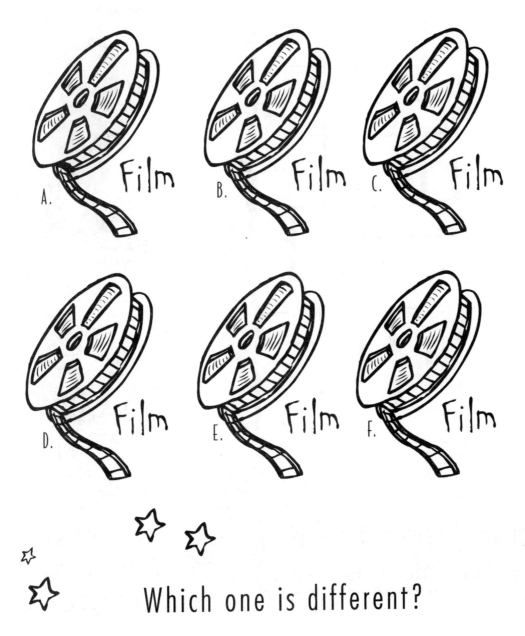

Which one is different?

FASTEST TALKER:

Steve Woodmore of Orpington, Kent, England, spoke 595 words in 56.01 seconds - a rate equivalent to 637.4 words per minute - on the ITV television program "MotorMouth" on September 22, 1990.

Stopwatch

How many words can you speak per minute? Have a friend time you.

Create your own personal record!

How many different movies have you watched? Have a contest with your family or friends. On a blank piece of paper write down all the names of the movies that you can remember watching. Take your time to think and remember. Record the winner with the most movies watched below.

(If you have seen a movie more than once, it only counts as one.)

★MY★ RECORD

MOST MOVIES WATCHED:

_____
NAME

_____ _____
NUMBER OF MOVIES WATCHED   DATE

GUINNESS WORLD RECORDS
MATCHING GAME
☆ ☆ ☆

BIGGEST ART COMPETITION.

Canvas

Easel

BIGGEST ART COMPETITION.

Canvas

Easel

Match!

You will find Guinness World Records Matching Cards on the next three pages . Color the pictures (make sure that the pairs match.) Cut out carefully along the dotted lines. Mix up the cards and place them face down on a playing surface. Turn over two cards. If they are the same, you have a match! If not, turn them back over. Keep trying two at a time. When you "match", remove them from the game while leaving the rest of the cards in their same place. The "wild" card matches any card. Keep track on a piece of paper of how many turns it takes to match all cards. This game can be played by yourself or with friends.

You can award the winner the "My Record".
(You can play this game as many times as you want until you feel a record has been set!)

★MY★ RECORD

MATCHING CHAMPION:

NAME

NUMBER OF MATCHES / NUMBER OF ATTEMPTS

DATE

BIGGEST ART COMPETITION.

BIGGEST ART COMPETITION.

MOST VALUABLE SLICE OF CAKE.

FASTEST DRUMMER.

FASTEST DRUMMER.

MOST VALUABLE SLICE OF CAKE.

BIGGEST BUBBLE GUM BUBBLE.

BIGGEST BUBBLE GUM BUBBLE.

BIGGEST HAMBURGER.

BIGGEST HAMBURGER.

MOST GRAND SLAMS.

MOST GRAND SLAMS.

HIGHEST GROSSING HORROR FILM.

HIGHEST GROSSING HORROR FILM.

MOST VALUABLE GUITAR.

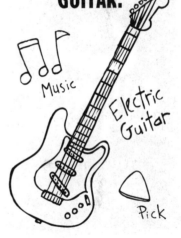

MOST VALUABLE GUITAR.

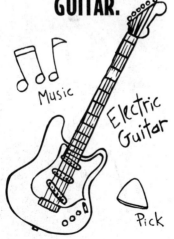

LARGEST PUMPKIN GROWN.

LARGEST PUMPKIN GROWN.

BIGGEST SHOE COLLECTION:

BIGGEST SHOE COLLECTION:

FIRST PERSON ON THE MOON:

Moon

FIRST PERSON ON THE MOON:

Moon

BIGGEST SIGNED BOOK COLLECTION:

☆ Book

BIGGEST SIGNED BOOK COLLECTION:

☆ Book

BIGGEST FRUIT STICKER COLLECTION:

Apple

BIGGEST FRUIT STICKER COLLECTION:

Apple

WILD CARD

Match!

GUINNESS WORLD RECORDS
Star Figure Logo

Redraw the Star Figure Logo, using the grid as a guide.

So you want to set a record too...

Do you think that you have what it takes to accomplish an extraordinary feat? If you do, read on.

Marbles

- Do you have a big collection of buttons, bottle caps or something else?
- Could you and your friends break the record for the biggest group hug?
- Could you try to break the record for the longest paper clip chain?

Safety first! Always tell a parent or adult before attempting any kind of record.

Why not set a brand new record?

To find out all the information about setting a record, visit the Guinness World Records web site: www.guinnessworldrecords.com
or write: Guinness World Records Ltd, 338 Euston Road, London NW1 3BD, United Kingdom.

Home Run!!
Bat
Ball
Music

GUINNESS WORLD RECORDS